# LONDON TERMINAL STATIONS IN THE 1960s

## David Christie

AMBERLEY

LNER A3 No. 4472 *Flying Scotsman* at Kings Cross at 23.30 on 31 August 1969, seen after returning from Newcastle on a LNER Society special – her last run before being shipped to the USA. The requisite bell and whistle for American use are prominent.

*Front cover upper*: A1 No. 60130 *Kestrel* arriving at Kings Cross on 2 March 1963.

*Front cover lower*: Western class D1000 *Western Enterprise* at Paddington on 5 September 1962.

*Back cover*: D200 at Liverpool Street on 31 August 1963.

First published 2018

Amberley Publishing
The Hill, Stroud
Gloucestershire, GL5 4EP

www.amberley-books.com

Copyright © David Christie, 2018

The right of David Christie to be identified as the Author of this work has been asserted in accordance with the Copyrights, Designs and Patents Act 1988.

ISBN 978 1 4456 7749 1 (print)
ISBN 978 1 4456 7750 7 (ebook)

British Library Cataloguing in Publication Data.
A catalogue record for this book is available from the British Library.

Origination by Amberley Publishing.
Printed in the UK.

# Contents

# Introduction

Starting at Kings Cross station on 3 September 1962, I unwittingly began my quest to record dying steam on BR. Having thought just to take a few frames in colour on my new 'Petri 7' camera at my old haunts from my schooldays, the subsequent large screen viewings of the projected slides were impressive enough to engender enthusiasm to want more. So it was that on 2 March 1963 (after the severe winter of 1962/3) I was back at Kings Cross to see and record more of my favourite A1s, A3s, and A4s. Unfortunately, at the age of twenty in 1963, resources were limited and colour film was expensive so it was a case of rationing my trips. Looking back at my notes taken at the time it is surprising how often I ran out of film on a trip. Digital photographers these days would be horrified!

Kings Cross (only until June 1963) Euston ( to end 1963) and Paddington (to end 1964) stations still had steam so were the favoured spots to visit, with Waterloo of course – but photography here was difficult with limited space at platform ends, so it took a back seat. Marylebone still had a few steam services, but St Pancras, Victoria and my 'home' Liverpool Street station were steamless. Victoria is included courtesy of my very first special and Liverpool Street manages to show a few of the more interesting diesels, such as D200. This station was used on every one of my rail trips, starting from Romford in Essex. It was on one 'normal' London visit in 1962 that the realisation dawned on me that there was no steam to be seen on my GE line, thus starting off my whole quest.

Being primarily concerned with capturing images of locomotives, the station buildings were somewhat overlooked – with limited 'under the roof' shots taken – due in most part to the reduced lighting and slowness of the colour films available, coupled with my Petri's maximum f2.8 aperture. This meant that the platform ends were the favoured spots, but of course one had to choose which platform carefully in order to get the subject clear, and this was not always achieved.

My earliest visits were generally with my nephew furiously taking down numbers, as I had done some five to ten years earlier. As is the way of things, starting work in 1959 brought about a change in priorities, blanking out my former railway interest for three years until the 'wake-up' call in '62. If that had not been the case, perhaps I should have been able to photograph my local Britannias and the Princess Royals at Euston. As it was, I just about managed a WR King (and only one).

Films used were Ektachrome (32asa) to start with, but soon changed to High-Speed Ektachrome (160asa), which was a bad decision; it ensured faster shutter speeds but at the expense of high grain and low saturation. From 1964 I changed to Kodachrome 64, which was generally good and served until 1967, when I switched camps to Agfa CT18 (50asa). My Petri camera saw out the decade, not to be replaced until 1971, when at last I was able to purchase an SLR. All slides were scanned on an Epson V800 scanner and corrected, for colour restoration mainly, on Photoshop. What cannot be corrected is sharpness, but I have included a few 'fuzzy' images where the shot is of interest.

Liverpool Street cab road entrance, which was my usual stance (on the sloping concrete strip) when trainspotting as a lad. This photograph was actually taken in May 1974, but it hadn't changed for decades.

# Kings Cross

My favourite London terminal, Kings Cross, was also the easiest to get around, my usual spot being on Platform 4/5, right by the signal box. York Road suburban platform was also used as it gave a good view of all the comings and goings. Kings Cross was also a regular departure point when visiting my Grannies at Welwyn in the '50s, and the ex-LNER Pacifics seen then impressed. I have a vivid memory of a long smokebox with a long nameplate and no deflectors – an A2/2 rebuild from Gresley's 2-8-2 P2 Class. Another exciting event here was finding the original Deltic diesel in its blue and silver livery – a sight for sore eyes indeed! Steam virtually vanished here overnight on 16 June 1963 with the commencement of the summer timetable, but later in the 1960s steam was seen again when special trains, generally hauled by *Flying Scotsman*, ran.

My first ever railway photograph, taken on 3 September 1962, with Class A4 No. 60028 *Walter K. Whigham* rather swamped by platform trolleys. She is in the usual excellent condition of Kings Cross Top Shed locos.

Underneath the large signal box, No. 60028 *Walter K. Whigham* now departs. This loco ran for only four more months in service.

Top Shed was in the habit of sending down its locos to the station two at a time. Here is No. A3 60110 *Robert the Devil* with A2 No. 60513 *Dante* behind. Waiting to depart on the adjacent track is A2 No. 60522 *Straight Deal*. This was another image from my first day, 3 September 1962.

A full view of A3 No. 60110 *Robert the Devil*, showing the double chimney and German-style smoke deflectors fitted a few years earlier. These came as something of a shock to me, being my first sight, and were definitely not an improvement to the A3's previous good looks.

It was now the turn of A2 No. 60522 *Straight Deal*, a York engine, to leave.

Diesels were in evidence, such as Deltic D9004, seen here in original condition, unnamed and without the yellow warning panel later applied. She would become *Queen's Own Highlander* in May 1964.

My last shot from my 3 September 1962 visit was of another un-panelled (yellow) diesel, and an unusual one at that, being prototype D0280 *Falcon* in an attractive two-tone livery. It is seen here departing with the Sheffield Pullman.

An across-the-platforms view of V2 No. 60869 arriving on a suburban train on my next visit to Kings Cross on 2 March 1963. The terrible state of the engine was typical of its home shed, New England.

A1 No. 60117 *Bois Roussel* is seen light engine on 2 March 1963, having been nicely turned out by Copley Hill shed.

Some Top Shed locos received the red-backed nameplate treatment, such as A4 No. 60015 *Quicksilver*, seen here on 2 March 1963 all ready to go, with the whistle (lovely chime!) being blown.

*Quicksilver* pulls away. She would be withdrawn just two months later.

A1 No. 60130 *Kestrel* arriving on 2 March 1963. Another Copley Hill A1, which seemed to rival Top Shed locos for cleanliness.

Not so clean, but then Grantham's V2 No. 60814 had arrived on a goods working. She was to be withdrawn in two months' time.

*Kestrel* stops briefly after release from her train.

No. 60130 now backs away into the shadow of the signal box. This is a good view of York Road platform.

The most famous of them all; A4 No. 60022 *Mallard*, a Top Shed loco, departs on 2 March 1963 in my final picture of that day. She was withdrawn in May 1963 for preservation, and is based at the National Railway Museum, York.

A3 No. 60107 *Royal Lancer,* another Top Shed loco, backs out on Good Friday, 12 April 1963.

Another doubling-up of light locos with A4 No. 60027 *Silver Fox* and A3 No. 60061 *Pretty Polly.*

Top Shed's A4 No. 60021 *Wild Swan* backs out, light engine, on 12 April 1963.

In complete contrast to the above, A2 No. 60520 *Owen Tudor* shows a typical New England mixture of rust and grime! It was an early departure, leaving for scrap three months hence.

A busy evening on Easter Saturday, 13 April 1963, with A3 No. 60061 *Pretty Polly* moving out while A1 No. 60114 *W. P. Allen* (Doncaster) waits to depart.

One of the first Brush Type 4s, D1510, allocated to Finsbury Park.

Doncaster's A1 No. 60156 *Great Central* departs on 13 April 1963.

New Brush Type 4 D1504 arrives on 27 April 1963.

Double-chimney V2 No. 60880 (New England) arrives on a non-corridor Peterborough train. This view was taken from York Road platform on Sunday 9 June 1963.

Another shot taken from York Road platform. English Electric Type 4 D275 arrives on a parcels train, also on 9 June 1963.

A2 No. 60500 *Edward Thomson* (New England) departs for Peterborough on 15 June 1963. This loco's withdrawal was just a matter of weeks away.

My last view of steam in service; A1 No. 60130 *Kestrel* waits to depart on 15 June 1963. Steam services finished at Kings Cross the next day, 16 June. Steam hadn't entirely vanished here just yet (apart from specials), as I witnessed on 17 August when A1 No. 60119 *Patrick Stirling* arrived one hour late, substituting for a failed diesel. Unfortunately, I was unable to photograph the event.

A steamless Kings Cross on 8 August 1964, with Deltic D9016 *Gordon Highlander* arriving.

Brush Type 2s galore with D5609, D5680 and D5853 lining up on 8 August 1964.

A 'Home Counties Railway Society' special on 4 October 1964 wasn't as expected. The loco booked for this train, bound for York, was a Duchess. However, nicely cleaned-up Britannia No. 70020 *Mercury* was a reasonable substitute.

*Mercury* departs. This Britannia would be a late withdrawal in January 1967.

LNER A3 No. 4472 *Flying Scotsman* backs out of Gas Works Tunnel on a lovely spring morning, 30 April 1967.

No. 4472 is seen here with her second tender, acquired in October 1966, which constituted a train, but requiring a brake van. *Flying Scotsman* propels this van into a siding.

A further manoeuvre, now without a van, to take the correct track for her train.

No. 4472 backs up amid the signals. Some railway workers look on with interest.

*Flying Scotsman* now departs – in a cloud, unfortunately! A railwayman records the event on either a Twin-Lens Reflex or a Box Brownie!

Another special with No. 4472 on 10 September 1967. A duller day and a closer shot as she backs down.

*Flying Scotsman* approaches her train in a scene remarkable for the lack of 'bodies' on the platform – unrepeatable today!

One week later, on 17 September 1967, GWR No. 7029 *Clun Castle* backs out of Gas Works Tunnel on another dull day. *Clun Castle* was, as far as I can recall, the only other 'preserved' loco to run at that time on BR tracks, at least locally.

*Clun* backs towards the platforms. She had required, unlike *Scotsman,* the minimum amount of livery change from her BR state – just the removal of her smokebox numberplate, the painting of '7029' on her buffer beam and the application of 'Great Western' on her tender. What hadn't been changed was her double chimney, fitted in 1959, but then it didn't seem to matter at the time! Later, in the 1980s, she was put back into her BR state (she was a BR-built engine in any case).

*Clun Castle* on her train, with a view over the platforms (more 'bodies' about, this time) to a full yellow front end Deltic.

The 'Ian Allan' special now departs, with my viewpoint above Gas Works Tunnel courtesy of notable photographer Brian Stephenson's ladder. This was gratefully used to climb a 10-foot-high wall to give us a superb view.

Another *Flying Scotsman* special out of 'The Cross', on an extremely wet 30 March 1969. No. 4472 backs down, with the effect accentuated by the weather conditions.

The A3 continues towards her train, passing underneath the signal box.

Using my high viewpoint again (this time no ladder was needed as gates in the wall were open) for a grand view of No. 4472 departing, surprisingly without a headboard. The photographers on York Road platform had to contend with being the wrong side of drifting smoke. At this time, 30 March 1969, the A3 was the only standard gauge steam loco to be allowed to use BR tracks – but not for long, as in September she would be on her way to the USA.

# Euston

Euston was totally different to Kings Cross, being a labyrinth of routes to the various platforms, which made it difficult to get around and see what was going on. During my photographic visits here the station was being rebuilt, with much demolition, including the infamous destruction of the Doric Arch. I well remember, in my 'spotting days, walking under this massive structure. My most vivid memory, however, was of the red Princess Royal locos, seemingly more impressive than their Duchess cousins. Unfortunately, the whole class had been withdrawn prior to my '62 visit, so I never managed to photograph one in BR service.

My visits ceased at the end of 1963, when steam was all but eliminated. At that time, electric wires and steam were not thought to be able to co-exist.

A case of being caught on the 'shade-side' at Euston. No. 46229 *Duchess of Hamilton* (Edge Hill) is seen arriving on the Emerald Isle Express on 5 September 1962. The loco is now owned by the NRM.

2MT No. 46424 on pilot work on 3 September 1962, and not long out of the shops judging by her appearance.

No. 46424 had a few years left to run, being scrapped in December 1966.

On the other end of the train, No. 46256 *Sir William A. Stanier* (Crewe North) backs out the empty stock of the Shamrock Express.

No. 46238 *City of Carlisle* (shedded at Carlisle) waits, on 5 September 1962, to take out a Perth express.

On Good Friday, 12 April 1963, Jubilee class No. 45717 *Dauntless* (Bank Hall) backs down onto her train.

A very grimy Fairburn 4MT Tank, No. 42068, banks out an outer suburban train. Note the LMS brake coach.

No. 46254 *City of Stoke-on-Trent* (Camden) backs out its train on 12 April 1963.

No. 46240 *City of Coventry* waits to depart on 18 May 1963. Much of the class was out of service in September 1964.

BR Standard 2MT No. 78039 shunts the Royal Mail coaches. This was a quick shot as I boarded my train on 25 May 1963, and it was taken for the coach interest – it's not often I don't get the whole loco in!

On my return to Euston, Britannia No. 70051 *Firth of Forth* (Crewe) was having trouble with its vacuum brakes on a returning FA Cup special.

No. 70051 was duly taken off to Camden shed and a Type 1 diesel was attached to test the vacuum.

Black 5 No. 45015 (Edge Hill) eventually backed down and the train left one hour late. Both locos were late survivors, lasting to December and September 1967 respectively.

No. 45015 departs into a setting sun on 25 May 1963.

Sunday 9 June 1963 and 8F No. 48416 is on a contractors' train, with the platform I had used for my first photographs here being demolished. The splendid red 'Euston' sign would not last much longer either.

Stanier 4MT Tank No. 42577 banks out an express. Another interesting ex-LMS brake coach can be seen here, and ex-works too!

Stanier 5MT 2-6-0 No. 42958 (Crewe) pulls out with the morning Royal Mail stock on 17 August 1963. This class was the poor relation of the 4-6-0 Black 5, and not often seen.

6 October 1963 and the station's destruction can be seen in the background as EE Type 4 D379 waits. Sulzer Type 2 D5074 is also in the shot.

Splendidly turned out No. 46245 *City of London* (Willesden) waits to depart with the LCGB Stanier Pacific Rail Tour on 17 November 1963. The gentleman in the cap and coat seemed to be worried about the front end, while a policeman chats to the driver.

*City of London*, all clear to go.

No. 46245 departs on her tour.

An unusual outfit for loco crew? Goodbye to the old Euston.

# Marylebone

Mostly nothing much happened at Marylebone when I used to call in on my rounds. Only two photographic visits were made, the first to see the last of the Royal Scots being used on the GC services, and the second to get my first sight of preserved LNER No. 4472 *Flying Scotsman* arriving on a special.

It is 19 October 1963 and Black 5 No. 44848 (Leicester) waits by stacks of parcels. She ran until February 1968.

There was a splendid view from the end of Marylebone's platform of the coaling and servicing areas for incoming locos. Here are two Royal Scots, Nos 46125 *Third Caribinier* (Willesden) and 46143 *South Staffs Regiment* (Annesley), both of which were in a pretty grimy state. They would only last another two months.

No. 46143 *South Staffs Regiment* on the turntable. Her number is only just discernible.

My first sight of LNER A3 No. 4472 *Flying Scotsman*, which had just arrived on a SLS tour on 18 April 1964.

Alan Pegler, the owner of No. 4472, being interviewed by a film unit immediately after *Flying Scotsman*'s arrival.

The film unit interviews Alan Pegler, to whose memory a great debt of gratitude is owed for being the first to preserve an express loco, and, in particular, such an iconic engine. That was in 1963 and these scenes present happier times for him, as an ill-fated visit with the engine to the USA in 1969 bankrupted him and almost stranded No. 4472 across the ocean. Happily for us rescue attempts were successful and, after having further owners, *Flying Scotsman* is now owned by the National Railway Museum and, albeit not in original form, still runs on the main line.

Most of the film crew head for the loco, which is now being turned on the turntable.

No. 4472 on her way round. This is how I would like to see her today, but disfiguring German-style smoke deflectors and a double chimney have been fitted, and as such the loco ran for the last few years in BR service.

On the evening of No. 4472's visit, green-liveried, double-chimeyed V2 No. 60963 (York) was at Marylebone's service area.

# Paddington

Paddington is my second favourite London terminal, after Kings Cross. There was always plenty going on here, with steam still being used for the station pilots. The Kings, Castles and Halls always (up until 1963) seemed to be smartly turned-out with their gleaming brass work and copper. On my photographic visits there was also more interest than usual in the new diesels with their Western uniqueness and varied liveries. The station itself was delightful, with its overall roof giving light and a good general view from the platform ends.

My first photograph at Paddington, on 5 September 1962, caught a King and a Castle together. No. 6000 *King George V* (Old Oak) is to the rear of No. 7027 *Thornbury Castle* (Worcester).

*Thornbury Castle* still survives and is undergoing restoration at a Weston-super-Mare works.

No. 6000 *King George V* departs, and was a shade too closely photographed (this was only my second day of railway photography). On withdrawal in February 1963 she passed into private ownership, spearheading the 'Return to Steam' tours in 1971. This was the first loco seen on BR tracks for two years following *Flying Scotsman*'s departure abroad. She is currently based at Steam, Swindon.

A Blue Pullman set arrives on 5 September 1962. There were only five sets built, and they were in service from 1960 to 1973.

A Blue Pullman set at the platforms.

Castle class No. 5058 *Earl of Clancarty* (Gloucester) is seen across the platforms on 5 September 1962.

Warship class D830 *Majestic* (Newton Abbot) arrives on the Torbay Express, complete with headboard.

The first Western class diesel, D1000 *Western Enterprise* (Old Oak), was a remarkable sight in its Desert Sand livery.

Brand-new D1037 *Western Empress* backs onto its train on 5 September 1962.

*Western Empress*'s lamp gets removed after coupling up.

Warship D830 *Majestic* gets ready to depart while Pannier tank No. 9453 passes on pilot duties on 5 September 1962.

No. 7914 *Lleweni Hall* (Reading) backs down.

After all those diesels it was nice to end the day with a Castle – and with a headboard too! No. 5041 *Tiverton Castle* (Old Oak) is ready to depart on the Cathedrals Express on 5 September 1962.

The only representative from my next visit on a wet 20 April 1963; No. 1506 was one of the unusual outside-cylinder Pannier tanks, and is seen here bringing in stock.

On an even wetter 9 June 1963, Standard Pannier tank No. 8433 pilots in.

On the same day, but in drier conditions, Pannier tank No. 9405 waits on pilot duties.

No. 7903 *Foremarke Hall* (Old Oak) arrives on 15 June 1963. This loco survived into preservation, and is now running on the Gloucestershire Warwickshire Steam Railway.

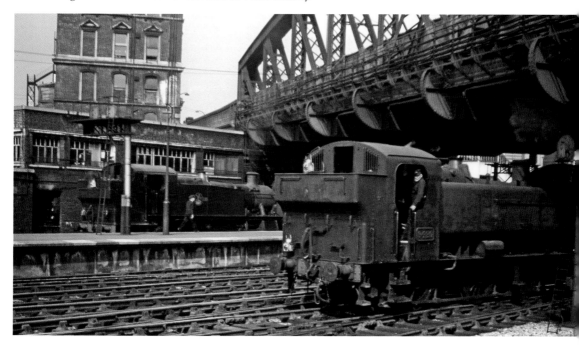

The tank engines on pilot duties are Pannier tank No. 9420 and 2-6-2T No. 6163.

2-6-2T No. 6163 again, with Pannier No. 3646 close to the camera.

2-6-2T No. 6135 completes the group of pilot engines in use on 15 June 1963.

A stranger under the roof at Paddington. Jubilee No. 45552 *Silver Jubilee* (Crewe North) was here for a special on 6 October 1963.

No. 45552 *Silver Jubilee* now departs with the Home Counties Railway Society special.

Pannier tank No. 8433 had possibly had a clean for piloting in the special's stock.

Pannier No. 8420 under the recently repainted overall roof on 6 October 1963.

Another special and a rare specimen for loco power, namely BR Standard No. 72006 *Clan Mackenzie* (Carlisle shed). This was on 8 December 1963 and was run by the prolific Home Counties Society again. Here, the Clan backs down.

No. 72006 is seen wreathed in steam at the head of her train. Unfortunately, she was positioned in just about the worst place – right under the road bridge.

The Clan, now with the headboard attached.

Ready for the 'off' – with a blast on her whistle.

*Clan Mackenzie* departs, being the focus for some youthful photographers.

Pannier tanks at the buffer stops on 8 December 1963. No. 9495 has been somewhat disfigured by the very ham-fisted application of its shed code!

Pannier tank No. 9415 with express-code lamps (!) on 28 March 1964.

A very surprising find on 28 March 1964 was a Castle, namely No. 7005 *Sir Edward Elgar* (Old Oak), being used on pilot duties! She had a pilot disc showing '3' on her lamp iron and had lost her front number plate, but retained her cabside number and nameplate.

2-6-2 Tank No. 6139 pulls out chocolate and cream stock on 18 April 1964. Just visible behind the loco is an LT Tube train. Surprisingly, these didn't normally coincide with a photographed BR train, and I never thought to capture one by itself.

Pannier No. 9710 was unusual in being fitted with condensing gear for working on LT lines. She is seen here on 8 August 1964.

More tank action with 2-6-2T No. 6160 on 8 August 1964. Tanks were the only steam now to be found at Paddington.

D1015 *Western Champion* (Laira), another loco in 'desert sand' livery, is seen arriving on 8 August 1964.

Warship D841 *Roebuck* (Newton Abbot), seen light engine, is released from its arrival on 8 August 1964.

An ex-GWR twelve-wheeled buffet car departing behind a Western diesel on 8 August 1964.

Condensing Pannier No. 9710 pilots in on 20 September 1964. Her smokebox number plate having been removed, her number has now appeared on her bufferbeam, GWR fashion.

Pannier No. 9710, captured from my carriage window. She was the last steam loco seen at Paddington and would be withdrawn just a few weeks later.

A taste of what was to come as, on 20 September 1964, experimental blue-liveried Brush Type 4 D1733 arrives. This loco was seen in June sporting red panels at each end, showing the double arrow BR insignia in white, but the panels had now been removed.

# Waterloo

This station was not one of my favourites, with photography being difficult at the platform ends. Most of my shots here were taken during rail trips to the IOW and the South West. I must admit to the Southern being the poor relation in my trainspotting days, and don't retain any specific memories of the station. Waterloo was the last London terminal to have steam, with 9 July 1967 being the last day.

Merchant Navy class No. 35001 *Channel Packet* (Nine Elms) backing out on a wet and gloomy 20 April 1963.

BR Standard 5MT No. 73089 (Nine Elms) departs on 20 April 1963.

A cheery wave from the driver as Merchant Navy No. 35009 *Shaw Savill Line* (Exmouth) departs on 9 June 1963. This loco survived to run on the East Lancs Railway.

My nephew looks on as West Country No. 34046 *Braunton* (Bournemouth) waits to depart on 9 June 1963. *Braunton* now runs on the West Somerset Railway.

Taken on my return from my first trip to the IOW, Unmodified West Country No. 34106 *Lydford* (Exmouth Junct.) departs on 25 April 1964. She was withdrawn within six months.

The sun at last! Merchant Navy No. 35024 *East Asiatic Co.* (Nine Elms), nicely clean, is seen at the head of a West Country train – on which I travelled, but only to Basingstoke. The date is 29 August 1964.

Warships were now to be seen at both Paddington and Waterloo. D826 *Jupiter* (Newton Abbot) waits to depart on 19 September 1964. This photograph was taken while on another trip to the IOW.

Early morning departures, taken from my train on yet another IOW trip. Clean Unmodified West Country No. 34102 *Lapford* (Eastleigh) is seen with not so clean No. 34006 *Bude* (Salisbury). The picture was taken on 11 October 1964.

As can be guessed from the headboard, this LCGB special was booked for a V2, but I was not too displeased to find a nicely turned-out Unmodified West Country No. 34002 *Salisbury* (Eastleigh) instead. This picture was taken on 3 July 1966.

BR Standard 5MT No. 73022 (Eastleigh), also seen on 3 July 1966.

Merchant Navy No. 35028 *Clan Line* (Nine Elms), now bereft of nameplates, waits at the head of my last BR steam-hauled journey on 29 April 1967, to Basingstoke. *Clan Line* only had three months to go before withdrawal, but was immediately bought for preservation and now runs specials on the network.

## Victoria

This was virtually a 'one-off' station for me, with the main event being my first special – and what a spectacle it was, with two locos in pre-Grouping liveries, and sunshine to boot! Victoria was an attractive setting, more so as this was a short train and well under the overall roof. For complete contrast, a later call-in was made to see the electric-hauled Golden Arrow.

A well turned-out U class No. 31639 (Norwood) at the buffers, having brought in the special's stock. The date was 15 September 1963.

Caledonian Railway 'Single' No. 123 heads LSWR 4-4-0 'T9' No. 120 on the Blue Belle, bound for the Bluebell Railway.

Probably the most elegant steam loco ever made, CR No. 123 releases steam, impatient to be off. The whitewashed coal is a nice touch, being the custom once for Royal trains.

LSWR T9 No. 120 also looked splendid, but not in the same league as her partner. The fitment of a larger boiler and smokebox in SR days made the application of the LSWR livery un-authentic. The straight-sided chimney would have once looked similar to CR No. 123's.

The T9 from the rear, with her huge eight-wheeled (inside-framed) tender prominent.

The special departs for Horsted Keynes, on the Bluebell line. No. 123 is now in the Glasgow Transport Museum but No. 120 is currently based at the Bodmin & Wenford Railway, on loan from the NRM, and is still running, albeit in BR livery.

On a very dull 28 March 1964, on the rounds of the stations with my nephew, a quick call-in at Victoria was made to see the Golden Arrow. Here, electric loco E5010 is seen departing. It was noted that the absolutely pristine Pullmans on the train were not matched by the loco's dirty state!

# Liverpool Street

My usual entry point into London, travelling the 15 miles from Romford, my home town. Liverpool Street was probably my most used location when trainspotting, the favourite spot being up the side of the taxi ramp, precariously perched on the sloping kerb. Despite the electric services to Shenfield (later to Southend), there still used to be steam-worked suburban trains via Bethnal Green to the north-east of London, so it was always busy and productive for number-taking youngsters. Favourite locos were the Britannias, which were new, in my time here. Unfortunately, steam finished quickest on the Great Eastern and, as previously mentioned, by the time I had started photography in September 1962, it had all gone. So my shots here are all diesels, taken en route to other destinations. There was a small sunlit section but I didn't manage to find it very often!

Five locos in shot here, the recognisable numbers being Brush Type 2 D5589 and EE Type 3 D6715. Photograph taken on 17 August 1963.

The first E Type 4, D200, with an early EE Type 3, D6703, on 31 August 1963. The first batch of EE Type 4s was introduced on the Great Eastern as one of the earliest main line diesel changeovers from steam and, like the Britannias before them, were kept in great condition.

BTH Type 1 D8234 with Brush Type 2 D5594 on 8 December 1963.

BTH Type 1 D8234, which was used as the station pilot, with EE Type 3 D6716 in the gloom of 8 December 1963.

D206 arriving on an even duller 14 March 1964.

BTH D8234 again – this time with a yellow panel applied. D200 is alongside on 28 March 1964.

D206 in a dark spot, but showing the sloping taxi ramp behind. The date is 8 August 1964.

A very much bulled-up Brush Type 2 D5620, with new headlights over the buffers. The painted vacuum pipes etc. would suggest its use on a special train? Photographed on 8 January 1967.